BANGKOK 2014

THE CITY AT A GLA

GW00836351

Mandarin Oriental

Superlative service and silky
made this Bangkok institutio
hotel for royalty and visiting
48 Thanon Charoen Krung/So

Assumption Cathedral

This Catholic cathedral was finished in 1821
to serve the city's French community, and was
rebuilt in the Romanesque style from 1910
to 1918. Its red-and-white brick facade stands
out among the modern towers along the river.
23 Soi Oriental, Thanon Charoen Krung

Jewelry Trade Center

Completed in 1995, this 221m high-rise,
designed by Urban Architects & Associates,
is the hub of Bangkok's booming gem trade.
The Silom Galleria in the lower plaza is a
retail space for art, antiques and jewellery.
919/1 Thanon Silom, T 02 630 0944

State Tower

Rangsan Architecture's overblown building,
with its dome, curved terraces and classical
motifs, was almost crippled by the 1997 Asian
financial crisis. However, since its opening in
2001 it has become an exclusive destination
and now attracts the city's beau monde.
1055 Thanon Silom

Chao Phraya

Choppy and clogged, Bangkok's snake-like
river swells with tugs, ferries, pleasure
cruisers, water taxis and local fishermen.

Shangri-La Hotel

The largest of the city's plush hotels opened in
1986 and seduces its guests into staying well-
and-truly put, thanks to six restaurants, a
luxurious spa and tropical riverfront gardens.
See p031

INTRODUCTION
THE CHANGING FACE OF THE URBAN SCENE

There's a media-fed familiarity to Bangkok, a coruscant whirl that takes in floating fruit markets, street vendors' sizzling hotplates and Buddhist stupas overlooking Patpong's floor shows. These days the city boasts an ever-growing skyline of megamalls and a futuristic transport system alongside crammed water taxis. It's a contradictory mix of new money and no money – luxury condos share area codes with corrugated-iron slums. These economic fault-lines are partly to blame for the unrest in 2010; the Central World mall was set on fire, but it has fully reopened – a sign for many that life has returned to normal. Thai politics have steadied, but for how long is anyone's guess, and with regular incidents, such as the 2011 floods, flux is the continuing theme of this resilient city.

Today's Bangkok smacks of sophistication – the Calatrava-style Rama VIII Bridge, the citywide planting of trees, even the tuk-tuks run on liquid propane. Schemes to promote creative industries have turned the city into a shoppers' paradise, and a swathe of chic new restaurants and bars is enabling it to justify its title as an Asian food capital. You can still do old-school Bangkok, living out hard-boiled noir subplots, ambling through riverside alleys, ogling scorpions at the pet market and swilling mojitos in five-star bars, trying to pick out the *hi-so* (high society) from the wannabes. It's your call, and the frisson produced by this choice is what makes Bangkok the beguiling temptress that she is.

ESSENTIAL INFO
FACTS, FIGURES AND USEFUL ADDRESSES

TOURIST OFFICE
Tourism Authority of Thailand
1600 Thanon Petchaburi
T 02 250 5500
www.tourismthailand.org

TRANSPORT
Airport transfer to city centre
airportraillink.railway.co.th
Trains depart regularly, from 6am to 12am.
The journey takes 30 minutes
BTS SkyTrain
T 02 617 7340
www.bts.co.th
MRT metro
T 02 624 5200
www.bangkokmetro.co.th
Metro and SkyTrains run from 6am to 12am
Taxis
Siam Taxi
T 1661
Cabs can be hailed on the street. Ask to
have the meter turned on

EMERGENCY SERVICES
Emergencies
T 191
Tourist police
T 1155
24-hour pharmacy
Foodland Supermarket Pharmacy
48 Column Tower, Sukhumvit Soi 16

EMBASSIES
British Embassy
14 Thanon Witthayu
T 02 305 8333
www.ukinthailand.fco.gov.uk
US Embassy
120-22 Thanon Witthayu
T 02 205 4000
bangkok.usembassy.gov

POSTAL SERVICES
Post office
Thanon Charoen Krung
T 02 614 7457
Shipping
DHL Express
1634/4 Thanon Petchaburi Tat Mai
T 02 684 8200

BOOKS
Architects 49 Ltd: Selected and
Current Works edited by Kate Ryan
and Eliza Hope (Images Publishing)
Classic Thai: Design Interiors
Architecture by Chami Jotisalikorn,
Phuthorn Bhumadhon and Virginia
McKeen Di Crocco (Tuttle Publishing)

WEBSITES
Architecture/Design
www.aecasia.com
Newspaper
www.bangkokpost.com

EVENTS
Bangkok International Design Festival
www.bangkokdesignfestival.com
International Festival of Dance & Music
www.bangkokfestivals.com

COST OF LIVING
Taxi from Suvarnabhumi International
Airport to city centre
THB350
Cappuccino
THB100
Packet of cigarettes
THB90
Daily newspaper
THB30
Bottle of champagne
THB6,000

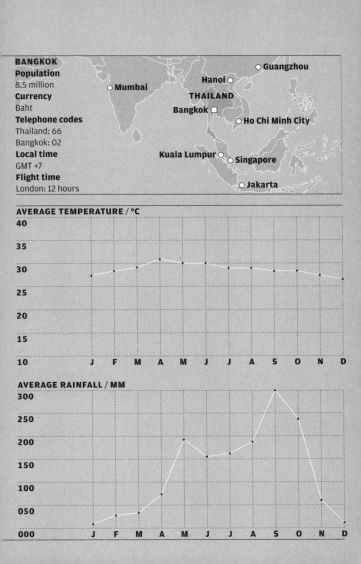

BANGKOK
Population
8.5 million
Currency
Baht
Telephone codes
Thailand: 66
Bangkok: 02
Local time
GMT +7
Flight time
London: 12 hours

○ Guangzhou
○ Mumbai
Hanoi ○
THAILAND
Bangkok □
○ Ho Chi Minh City
Kuala Lumpur ○
○ Singapore
○ Jakarta

AVERAGE TEMPERATURE / °C

```
40

35

30

25

20

15

10
     J   F   M   A   M   J   J   A   S   O   N   D
```

AVERAGE RAINFALL / MM

```
300

250

200

150

100

050

000
     J   F   M   A   M   J   J   A   S   O   N   D
```

NEIGHBOURHOODS
THE AREAS YOU NEED TO KNOW AND WHY

To help you navigate the city, we've chosen the most interesting districts (see below and the map inside the back cover) and colour-coded our featured venues, according to their location; those venues that are outside these areas are not coloured.

CHATUCHAK

In the north of the city, the wooden sprawl of the world-famous Chatuchak Weekend Market (or 'JJ') is on the edge of the little-known Chatuchak Park. Whisking you out here are the SkyTrain and the MRT, the latter more convenient for the market. Nearby, you'll also find one of the best selections of fresh produce in Bangkok, at the Or Tor Kor Market (Thanon Kamphaeng Phet), and vibrant, if off-the-radar, nightlife.

OLD TOWN

Where the wide lanes of Thanon Sathorn reach the nut-brown Chao Phraya river, hotels such as the Mandarin Oriental (see p016) and the Shangri-La (see p031) rise up with an imperious garishness. Further north, the sector that contains old wooden Chinese architecture and teems with noodle vendors marks the de facto Old Town. It's a mix of the ancient and the bustling modern, from hidden Hokkien coffee shops to boutique fashion stores.

SUKHUMVIT

This traffic-clogged, mall-mobbed avenue goes on for miles. It contains plenty of trendy sub-sections, whether that be leafy lanes such as Soi 31, with its furniture and fashion studios, or urban it-spots such as Thong Lor and Ekkamai (Soi 63) – all neighbourhoods unto themselves. Many eating, drinking and dancing hotspots are found around here, including Quince (see p038) and Long Table (see p060).

SIAM

Students, high-haired society wives and international models all flock to this shopping and youth-culture hub. They flow between air-conditioned malls on Thanon Rama I, such as Siam Paragon (No 991, T 610 8000) and Siam Center (Siam Tower, T 2658 1000), and the neon-lit lanes to the south. Rummaging in backstreet stalls will yield cheap jewellery and even a deco cinema, the Scala Theatre (T 02 251 2861).

SILOM/SATHORN

South-west of the city's main green lung, Lumphini Park (see p014), this is the one part of Bangkok with a linear concentration of skyscrapers, including the idiosyncratic Robot Building (see p013) and financial-powerhouse offices. The area's focus tends to be the pedestrianised Thanon Silom and its sister side roads, Convent and Sala Daeng, lined with gay bars, dance halls, destination eateries, such as D'Sens (see p042), and lady-boy cabarets.

ROYAL CITY AVENUE

Once a students-only realm, with lurid massage parlours tucked down the nearby alleys, the RCA district has undergone a rapid facelift. The city *officially* shuts down at 2am but RCA is regularly open at least an hour later, and a fresh generation of visionary owners have created a nightlife centre with a wide range of clubs, including the vast dance palace Flix RCA (29/22-32 Royal City Avenue, T 081 645 1188).

LANDMARKS
THE SHAPE OF THE CITY SKYLINE

Bangkok is a textbook example of urban Asian sprawl. It has many concrete, six-lane avenues in the wrong parts of town and single-lane avenues in the right ones. But with good planning, it can be packaged into work, shop and play zones and managed accordingly.

Retail outlets are mainly concentrated on one long, smoggy drag that begins on Thanon Rama I, by Siam Square, and unfurls east along the path of the SkyTrain, joining Thanon Sukhumvit near the seedy Nana Plaza complex. Sukhumvit's *soi* (side lanes) are like mini-neighbourhoods; key streets include Soi 63, or Ekkamai, hub of the party scene; Soi 55, aka Thong Lor, home to high-end shopping centres J Avenue (No 15), and Duangrit Bunnag's H1 (see p065); and Soi 11, which offers a complete night out on one strip.

The 2001 State Tower (1055 Thanon Silom), a 247m landmark designed by Thai firm Rangsan Architecture, sits at the edge of the Old Town, which encompasses wooden shophouses, noodle-store-filled alleys and temples like Wat Pho (Thanon Chetuphon) and the Royal Grand Palace (Thanon Na Phra Lan) along the Chao Phraya's banks. The other areas to visit are Silom and Sathorn, a mash-up of offices, swish hotels, quaint side streets, A-list eateries and the sleaze of Patpong. Above all of this, the MahaNakhon Building is rising; when OMA's mostly residential tower is finally finished in 2014, it will be Bangkok's tallest structure, at 313m high. *For full addresses, see Resources.*

CAT Building

The head office of CAT Telecom, this 35-floor tower sits on the edge of the Chao Phraya, from where it beams radio waves across the city. It's the kind of lumpen, glass-and-steel office block that gives new Asian architecture such a bad name, but it does make a useful reference point along the river, near the distinctive dome of the State Tower (right; see p009).
72 Thanon Charoen Krung

Dusit Thani

The tallest building in the city for at least a few months after its opening in 1970, this hotel is a rare project, reflecting art deco and modernist influences in a way that is distinctly Thai. Striking at night, when the geometrical, gold-lined frames that run up the structure are lit, the hotel is symbolic to Bangkok residents because it is locally owned and was one of the first buildings here to make a high-rise statement. For expats, the way in which the Dusit Thani has melded Eastern elements in a Western modernist context makes for a point of conversation. Note the influence of Buddhist architecture in the portico-like frames and shape of the structure. Lumphini Park (see p014) is within a few steps of its doors.
946 Thanon Rama IV, T 02 200 9000, www.dusit.com

Robot Building

At ground level, there is not a great deal to distinguish the Bangkok headquarters of the United Overseas Bank (UOB) from any other high-rise lining the gridlocked Thanon Sathorn. However, viewed from afar (the SkyTrain between Surasak and Chong Nonsi stations, say), architect Sumet Jumsai's 83m-high structure jumps out. Tagged the 'Robot', it was inspired by one of his son's toys and was completed in 1986. The staggered shape rises through 20 floors, its 6m-diameter 'eyeballs' of reflective glass forming windows, hooded by metal-louvred 'eyelids'. The rooftop communication antennae double up as lightning rods and the 'caterpillar wheels' and reinforced concrete 'nuts' adorning the building also have a practical function as unusual window casings and sunshades.
191 Thanon Sathorn Tai

Lumphini Park
Commissioned by King Rama VI, whose
statue (pictured) guards an entrance,
this park opened to the public in the
1920s and is the city's one true, readily
used expanse of grass, with ponds and
shady paths. Backgammon is played
under pagodas, and locals engage in
aerobics, badminton, ballroom dancing,
and *sepak takraw* (kick volleyball).
Thanon Rama IV

HOTELS

WHERE TO STAY AND WHICH ROOMS TO BOOK

If there is any single business that benefits from the no worries/all smiles Thai approach to life and the fluid grace of Buddhist society, it is hospitality. First-time visitors to Bangkok are often drawn to the tranquillity of the river, where colonial-style five-star choices abound, from the local grande dame, the Mandarin Oriental (48 Thanon Charoen Krung/Soi 38, T 02 659 9000), to the opulent Shangri-La (see p031). Other riverside options are The Peninsula (333 Thanon Charoen Nakhon, T 02 861 2888) and the Millennium Hilton (123 Thanon Charoen Nakhon, T 02 442 2000); for a more intimate experience, try the elegant Arun Residence (see p020).

Downtown, there's been a trend towards design-conscious refits, such as at Hotel Muse (55/555 Soi Lang Suan, T 02 630 4000), where interiors are a mash-up of the golden King Rama V era and turn-of-the-century fin de siècle; and Luxx XL (82/8 Soi Lang Suan, T 02 684 1111), a 51-room conversion of a seven-storey building, which has a 12m infinity pool. The global economic crisis didn't halt the arrival of several new hotels. In 2012 the W (106 Thanon Sathorn Nua, T 02 344 4000) opened, as did the Sofitel Sukhumvit (189 Sukhumvit Soi 13-15, T 02 126 9999), following the launch of its luxe sister property, Sofitel So (see p028). In 2015, the MahaNakhon Building (see p009) will house a 150-room Edition, a collaboration between Ian Schrager and Marriott.
For full addresses and room rates, see Resources.

Cabochon Hotel

Although the interiors of this four-suite, four-studio hotel may appear convincingly aged, it actually only opened its doors in 2012. Propelling the city's current trend for boutique hotels with period aesthetics, owner and interior designer Eugene Yeh has paid extraordinary attention to detail to immerse guests in a time capsule of 1920s Shanghai; a place where filmmaker Wong Kar-Wai's imagination might roam.

Bedlinen was flown in from Belgium, vanity mirrors are set in antique wooden frames, and the suites (above), have large living rooms. The commitment to authenticity continues at the Joy Luck Club, the in-house cocktail bar filled with models of classic airplanes, vintage Louis Vuitton trunks and a dusty set of books. *14/29 Sukhumvit Soi 45, T 02 259 2871, www.cabochonhotel.com*

The Siam

Reviving a long-established penchant for riverside accommodation, The Siam, opened in 2012, sits on a 1.2-hectare plot banking the Chao Phraya, just north of the Rama VIII Bridge. Owner Krissada Sukosol Clapp is known locally for his pop music and film roles, but on show here is his impressive collection of antiques and curios – including everything from dentist chairs to French horns suspended above the chequered tiles of the dapper Deco Bar & Bistro. Architect and designer Bill Bensley has introduced muted tones of black, grey and white with art deco accents, as seen in the lobby area (above). Positioned around frangipani-shaded courtyards, each of the 39 unique suites and pool villas is serviced by a butler.
3/2 Thanon Khao, T 02 206 6999, www.thesiamhotel.com

Arun Residence

Portuguese-colonial-style architecture coexists with Ratanakosin-era art at this boutique hotel. The renovation of a former waterfront warehouse was overseen by Thai architect and interior designer Chavalit Chavawan, who has created a simply decorated, two-storey, seven-room hideaway by the Chao Phraya river. We recommend you plump for the spacious Roof Garden Suite (right). Outside the air-conditioned rooms it can get rather stuffy, but this only adds to the authentic ambience – the hotel is located in a tiny one-lane *soi* filled with numerous shophouses selling everything from metal panelling to rice. The breathtaking views of Wat Arun (see p034) are best enjoyed at sunrise and at dusk, while enjoying Thai fusion cuisine at The Deck restaurant on Arun's wooden veranda.

36-38 Soi Pratoo Nok Yoong,
T 02 221 9158, www.arunresidence.com

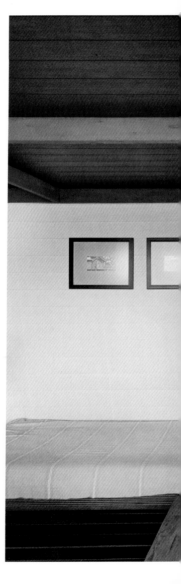

Siam Kempinski Hotel

Opened in 2010, this 303-room city resort sits on land that was formerly part of the neighbouring Sra Pathum Palace, current home of Princess Maha Chakri Sirindhorn. Throughout the resort's eclectic interiors, provided by Hirsch Bedner Associates, the lotus is omnipresent, dominating a series of photos by Dow Wasiksiri in each guest room. Local firm Tandem Architects designed a horseshoe layout, where all rooms look on to landscaped tropical gardens of Thai flora and three saltwater pools. The 106 sq m Garden Suite (above) features a luxurious working area, a sleek marble bathroom and direct access to the unfeasibly quiet gardens, which contrast with the bustling city centre just beyond the property's walls. Visit the hotel's authentic Thai restaurant, Sra Bua, and the poolside Rotunda bar (opposite).
991/9 Thanon Rama I, T 02 162 9000, www.kempinski.com

Siam@Siam Design Hotel & Spa
This 203-room hotel with an extensive
spa opened in 2007, its bold orange-
and-blue facade contrasting with the
raw concrete walls and steel accents
favoured by interior designer Kittisak
Suthammachote. Rooms, such as
the Grand Biz Class (pictured), feature
abstract paintings by local artists.
865 Thanon Rama I, T 02 217 3000.
www.siamatsiam.com

Metropolitan by COMO

Christina Ong's urban hostelry is a former YMCA, and its featureless architecture was used as a blank canvas, as you may detect from the lobby (above). The exterior is lit in glowing panels by Isometrix's Arnold Chan, so the double-height duplex Penthouse Suites are as alluring from the outside as they are within. Staff flit about in Comme des Garçons threads, and rooms feature yoga mats and teak lotus chairs; we suggest you opt for the Terrace Room which has a semi-outdoor shower. Darkwoods offset a Zen-touched, stark minimalism in the COMO Shambhala Spa, but note that sunlight doesn't hit the blue-tiled pool until around lunchtime. Chef David Thompson's Thai restaurant, Nahm (see p050), opened here in 2010. *27 Thanon Sathorn Tai, T 02 625 3333, www.comohotels.com/metropolitan*

Chakrabongse Villas

This urban retreat takes its name from a Thai prince, who commissioned these Ayutthaya-style stilted wooden villas for entertaining in the early 20th century. The seven suites, which include the Thai House, the Riverside Villa, the Garden Suite (above) and the Chinese Suite, have an intimacy that recalls European-esque inns on a good day. The villas have luxe beds, polished floors, darkwood fittings and traditional furnishings. Among the amenities are a 10m pool, a chef who goes to market every day and a private boat mooring. As with the Arun Residence (see p020), you can see Wat Arun across the river and, unlike many five-star waterfront hotels, there's a sense of engagement with the rituals and rhythms of daily Thai life.
396 Thanon Mahathat, T 02 222 1290, www.thaivillas.com

Sofitel So
Christian Lacroix provided the finishing touches to the quiff-like, 30-storey Sofitel So, designed by Thai architect Smith Obayawat. Its 238 rooms and suites are based on the five elements; Water rooms, for example, have bathtubs with epic views, whereas Woods (So Lofty Room, pictured) feature teak panelled walls. A 10th-floor infinity pool overlooks Lumphini Park.
2 Thanon Sathorn Nua, T 02 624 0000

Dream

Converted in 2006 from an existing building by Bent Severin, this boutique hotel is owned by socialite Vikram Chatwal. The interiors, by Bangkok firm ASC, follow a modern, East-meets-West aesthetic; the lobby features replicas of the mound-like *chedi* found in Buddhist temples. The 195 rooms are bathed in a relaxing blue-hued light from recessed fluorescent tubes situated in glass desktops and under the platform beds, as in the stylish Dream Suite 807 (above). Techno-furnishings include an iPod Nano, a DVD player, free wi-fi and a 42in plasma TV. Dream is popular with creative types who appreciate the high-quality service, the restaurant/lounge Flava and the rooftop pool parties in the Dream 2 wing.
10 Sukhumvit Soi 15, T 02 254 8500, www.dreambkk.com

Shangri-La Hotel

The 802-room Shangri-La, which opened in 1986 and was given a £37m makeover in 2009, has enough facilities to make you feel as if you need never leave. Indeed, many of its guests shuttle only between their rooms and their respective business meetings in the city. The accommodation, divided between two wings, is plush, well equipped and comfortable – we were taken with the view from the Speciality Suite. The complex's six restaurants serve Thai, Cantonese, Italian and global fare, and there are three bars. Recuperate in the health club or the CHI spa, where the 107 sq m Garden Suite has an outdoor infinity bath set in a lotus pond. Also look out for the swimming pools hidden among the manicured, if slightly twee, gardens. *89 Soi Wat Suan Plu, T 02 236 7777, www.shangri-la.com/bangkok*

24 HOURS
SEE THE BEST OF THE CITY IN JUST ONE DAY

Two decades ago, Bangkok had fewer than 100 7-Eleven stores and not a public-transport system or eight-lane highway in sight. The thought of trying to see the city in 24 hours would send shudders through wide-eyed tourists and knowing locals alike. A three-hour trip from the airport was normal, and it took two hours to get from Lumphini Park (see p014) to Chinatown. But things have changed. Now, as well as the old methods of transport, such as boats and motorbikes, there's the MRT and the SkyTrain, and an airport rail link connects to BTS Phaya Thai station, high above the congestion.

The City of Angels is one of extremes and to explore it properly you should experience them all: on land and on water; from high society down to grass-roots level; and from the royal palaces to the dizzying, fume-filled streets. This means greeting the day with a coffee, perhaps at the refined Erawan (opposite), before a trip down the Chao Phraya. Above all, it means having fun and not forgetting to relax; if the boat ride doesn't do it, then a massage at Ruen-Nuad (Second floor, 42 Thanon Convent, T 02 632 2662), surely will. If your schedule permits, head north to the Museum of Contemporary Art (499 Moo 3 Thanon Vibhavadi Rangsit, T 02 953 1005), then end the day with dinner at a style-conscious eaterie, such as Quince (see p038). This is the land of *sanuk* (which loosely translates as 'fun') and *mai pen rai* ('don't worry').
For full addresses, see Resources.

10.00 Erawan Tea Room

On the second floor of the stylish Erawan Bangkok shopping mall, Erawan Tea Room is a legendary 1960s venue, where Jackie Kennedy is reputed to have dined. The interior, with its warm orange tones and Thai-Chinese detailing, was reinvented by designer Tony Chi. It's a pleasant place for morning coffee. Sit near the windows, if you can, which overlook the Erawan Shrine, a gilded statue erected in the 1950s to appease the land gods during the building of the Erawan Hotel, which subsequently became the Grand Hyatt Erawan (T 02 254 1234). If you're more partial to tea than coffee, you can choose from Indian, Sri Lankan, Chinese or Thai varieties (the teas are also available in packages so you can take them away). *494 Thanon Phloen Chit, T 02 250 7777, www.erawanbangkok.com*

12.00 Wat Arun

Two different faces of Bangkok can be seen on the banks of the Chao Phraya, where Sino-Portuguese shophouses look across to gleaming, modern hotels. Take a river taxi from Saphan Taksin pier for the 15-minute ride to Tha Tien, past locals fishing for their dinners. From here, an express boat will ferry you to Wat Arun. Construction began during the Ayutthaya era (1350-1767), although the towering central prang, which is surrounded by four smaller ones, wasn't added until the 19th century. Wat Arun translates as the 'Temple of the Dawn', and earned its name from the way light shimmers off its stucco-covered surface. This exterior is decorated with porcelain that Chinese ships used as ballast before discarding. *34 Thanon Arun Amarin, T 02 891 1149*

14.30 TCDC

Opened in 2005, the Thailand Creative & Design Center (TCDC) hosts eclectic exhibitions, and its library (above) has more than 15,000 titles covering all aspects of design, including art history, architecture, fashion and photography. Duangrit Bunnag created the space, using a gold motif typically seen in Thai temples, as well as local teak for the bookshelves. When you're done with the culture, have lunch at Greyhound Café (T 02 664 8663), on the second floor. The Greyhound brand is known throughout Thailand for its fashion collections, but here its sister company, Sweet Hound, presents a dessert menu featuring delights such as the banoffee pie, where caramel, bananas and cream are served up in a jar. *Sixth floor, Emporium Shopping Complex, T 02 664 8448, www.tcdc.or.th*

16.30 Bangkok Art and Culture Centre

For a taste of contemporary art and design, head to the publicly funded BACC. After years of planning disputes and several changes in government, the centre finally opened in 2008. But it was only in 2012, thanks to some high-profile and well-attended exhibitions, that the 10-storey, 7,600 sq m hub carved its niche in a city that can, at times, be creatively decentred. Designed by architect Robert Boughey, the building is reminiscent of the New York Guggenheim's corkscrewed interior, mixed with the familiarity of a shopping centre. Inside, find everything from locally produced handicrafts in modest artist-run shops on lower levels, to internationally acclaimed artworks in the exhibition halls on the top three floors.

939 Thanon Rama I, T 02 214 6630, www.bacc.or.th

20.00 Quince

In a converted house that oozes rustic charm, Quince is the latest venue in which pan-Mediterranean food sets the agenda, attracting a well-heeled crowd in the process. The front room is an industrial-style glass-walled cube with moody lighting; the back room (pictured) has more intimate seating under a vintage Barnum & Bailey circus poster.
Sukhumvit Soi 45, T 02 662 4478

URBAN LIFE
CAFÉS, RESTAURANTS, BARS AND NIGHTCLUBS

Bangkok has shed its reputation for being a sleazy throng of go-go bars and sexpats. It's now one of South-East Asia's most vibrant cities in which to eat, drink, dance and all combinations thereof. From world-class street hawkers selling grilled meats, noodles and dishes prepared *à la minute*, to the raft of great global choices, Bangkok is an epicurean paradise for all tastes and budgets.

Westerners congregate in the expanding Sukhumvit Soi 11, at venues such as the Peruvian fusion kitchen Above Eleven (33rd floor, Frasier Suites Sukhumvit, 38/8 Sukhumvit Soi 11, T 02 207 9300), but monied locals prefer to frequent the latest hotspots on Ekkamai and Thong Lor, where bar-chitect Ash Sutton's Fat'r Gut'z (Seenspace, 251/5 Thong Lor Soi 13, T 02 185 2378) serves up fish and chips along with five-star cocktails. Gay Bangkok, meanwhile, centres on Silom Soi 2 and 4, and the bars and clubs of reborn nightlife district Royal City Avenue (RCA) stay open late, their Top Ten soundtracks attracting a youthful crowd.

Also popular is the Old Town and its cluster of European-style bars on Thanon Phra Athit, near the backpackers' ghetto around Thanon Khao San. In the centre, chef Ian Kittichai's Hyde & Seek (65/1 Athenee Residence, Soi Ruamrudee, Thanon Witthayu, T 02 168 5152) mixes some of the city's best cocktails. Across town, Soi Ari is booming due to design-conscious venues like Salt (see p059). *For full addresses, see Resources.*

Soul Food Mahanakorn

For hip, hearty and local food, try Soul Food, a three-storey shophouse near the mouth of Thong Lor. As the name suggests, the restaurant serves comfort food in a cosy setting. Highlights include *khao soi*, a mild northern curry with crunchy noodles; and *mieng kham*, lettuce leaves in which to wrap chilli, lime, peanuts and tamarind sauce. Rotating specials keep things fresh. Owner Jarrett Wrisley, a food writer turned restaurateur, designed the space and will squeeze you in upstairs if the main room (above) is full, which it often is. Works by local artists line the panelled walls and simple Scandinavian-style furniture sits on polished concrete floors. Potent cocktails and on point music keep the steady expat crowd happy. *56/10 Sukhumvit Soi 55, T 02 714 7708, www.soulfoodmahanakorn.com*

D'Sens
Since 2004, foodies have flocked to
D'Sens, an outpost of Michelin-starred
chefs Jacques and Laurent Pourcel,
whose French cuisine has Thai and
Mediterranean influences. Set on the
top floor of the Dusit Thani (see p012),
the recently renovated restaurant's
views are as impressive as its food.
*Dusit Thani, 946 Thanon Rama IV,
T 02 200 9000; www.dusit.com*

Bamboo Chic Bar

Although predominantly a place to have a drink, Bamboo Chic Bar, in Le Méridien hotel, offers a range of inventive snacks, including a modern spin on the Japanese speciality of *robata* (skewered food slow-cooked over charcoal). However, the main star of the show is the extensive selection of sakes, wines and signature cocktails; order the Bamboo Crush with Chivas Regal, ginger ale and apple juice. Opened in 2008, Bamboo Chic's interiors, by Orbit Design Studio, feature two huge Egyptian crystal chandeliers and an underlit walkway that guides guests through the dark entrance. Elsewhere in the hotel, Latest Recipe restaurant serves up hearty breakfasts devised by Michelin-starred New York-based chef Jean-Georges Vongerichten.
Fourth floor, Le Méridien,
40/5 Thanon Surawong, T 02 232 8888,
www.lemeridienbangkokpatpong.com

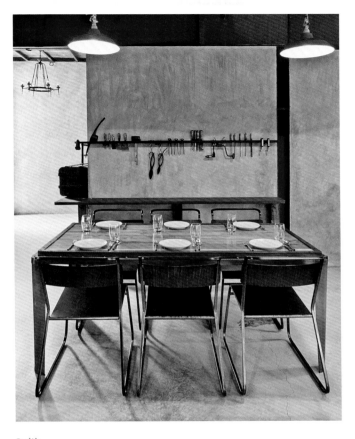

Smith

If Thailand has a celebrity chef, it is Ian Kittichai, whose reach stretches from New York to Mumbai, and all over Bangkok. His 2012 opening, Smith, is a carnivore's paradise (and a vegetarian's nightmare), delivering nose-to-tail European recipes made with locally sourced produce. It's a bold move in an increasingly health-conscious, image-obsessed city, although offal has always been served in Thai street kitchens. An outdoor area (opposite) offers a quiet alternative to the usually bustling main room (above), where macabre racks of tools hang on internal walls. If it's on offer, order the spicy haggis, or slow-cooked lamb, and enjoy the sight of the city's elite chomping on cheap cuts of meat in a former storage warehouse.
1/8 Sukhumvit Soi 49, T 02 261 0515,
www.smith-restaurant.com

Sirocco

This sleek venue takes its name from the Mediterranean wind, and serves a selection of dishes from the same region. Perched 209m up on the 63rd floor of the State Tower, Sirocco has a skywalk stretching out over the city, on which there is a circular bar (pictured), serving fine wine and premium vodka.
Lebua at State Tower, 1055 Thanon Silom, T 02 624 9999, www.lebua.com

Nahm

The original incarnation of Nahm in London's Halkin hotel was the first Thai restaurant to win a Michelin star. In 2010, its chef, David Thompson, opened this Bangkok outpost at the Metropolitan by COMO (see p026), causing much debate about whether a *farang* (Westerner) could cook authentic Thai food. He has proved the doubters wrong. Many of Thompson's dishes, such as smoked fish curry with prawns, chicken livers and cockles, and stir-fried frogs' legs, are based on recipes from the Thai royal court, and desserts are by Thompson's long-time partner, chef Tanongsak Yordwai. Designer Koichiro Ikebuchi's layout gives a subtle nod to Thai heritage, featuring teak floors and gold-leaf, and overlooks an outdoor pool. *Metropolitan by COMO, 27 Thanon Sathorn Tai, T 02 625 3333, www.comohotels.com*

Nest

Concealed among a forest of skyscrapers, the chilled-out hotel restaurant/bar Nest is an open-air oasis in the clubland of Sukhumvit Soi 11. Opened in 2008, the garden setting, complete with Shera wood decking and tropical plants, is a great spot in which to kick back on one of the curved-frame beds. The menu is a mishmash of Thai, Western, Asian fusion and tapas-style dishes – unusual outside the five-star hotels – and, as for cocktails, we recommend The Thailander (sour-and-spicy *tom yam*, vodka, lime and coconut liquor). In the event of inclement weather, a 50m retractable canvas roof extends over the terrace. Nest is popular with expats, fashionable locals and disco divas alike.
Ninth floor, Le Fenix Sukhumvit,
33/33 Sukhumvit Soi 11, T 02 255 0638,
www.thenestbangkok.com

Bo.lan

Former students of David Thompson, the Michelin-starred chef at Nahm (see p050), Duangporn Songvisava (Bo) and Dylan Jones (lan) opened Bo.lan in 2009. The name is also a play on the Thai word *boran*, meaning 'ancient', and the menu would not be out of place in the courts of the Sukhothai and Ayutthaya periods. The fragrant, delicate taste of dishes such as *dtom klong*, a hot soup with smoked fish, and stir-fried squid with palm heart and red chillies, expertly showcase the impressive breadth of Thai cooking. The interior is adorned with lampshades fashioned out of *gra dong* (traditional flat baskets made from bamboo used for drying chillies and fish) and a rotating selection of exquisite Thai artwork.
42 Soi Pichai Ronnarong, Sukhumvit Soi 26, T 02 260 2962, www.bolan.co.th

Bed Supperclub
Its white interior and curvaceous take on industrial design have made this tubular structure something of an archetypal venue for modern Bangkok. You can dine horizontally in the restaurant, choosing from a Mediterranean-Asian menu, and then boogie vertically in the adjoining club.
26 Sukhumvit Soi 11, T 02 651 3537, www.bedsupperclub.com

Tables

Situated on the mezzanine of the five-star Grand Hyatt Erawan, in a space designed by Tony Chi, Tables has an Old-World atmosphere, evoked by 1900s-style travertine tiled floors, oxidised mirrors and leather burgundy couches. But there's also a nod to the Asian aesthetic, thanks to rattan partitions and a plush ceiling of deep-red bamboo. Swiss chef Michel Eschmann's European menu, which has French leanings, offers steak *au poivre* and dover sole *meunière*, and about half of the dishes can be executed tableside on specially designed hobs. The Sunday brunch is particularly popular; expect to dine alongside politicians, high-powered executives and serious local gourmands.
Grand Hyatt Erawan, 494 Thanon Ratchadamri, T 02 254 1234, www.bangkok.grand.hyatt.com

WTF Gallery & Cafe

Big-budget projects may form the obvious peaks of urban life in Bangkok, but the independent venues more than fill any gaps in-between with their own creative agendas. Since 2010, the shophouse confines of WTF has teemed with the city's in-the-know creatives, who gather here for regular events – from poetry readings and exhibitions to pop-up kitchens. Co-owner Christopher Wise is responsible for the design, which combines retro Thai movie posters on wooden panelling with cosy nooks in which to enjoy the small selection of tapas, and a gallery upstairs that showcases work from artists who are mainly Bangkok-based. Drop by for one of the tasty, zippily named signature cocktails, such as the Muay Thai Punch.
7 Sukhumvit Soi 51, T 02 662 6246, www.wtfbangkok.com

Salt

Leafy Soi Ari is about as close as Bangkok gets to being bohemian and it bustles with boutiques, coffee shops and young arty types. Salt opened in 2011 and sits on the quiet corner of Soi 4. Designer Antika Teparak converted this concrete shell of a former sales office into a minimalist glass box, with floor-to-ceiling windows, a marble bar and a terrace with a small rock garden. A lounge area was added in 2012. The cuisine is a mix of Japanese, Italian and French with a local twist — think carpaccio with a Thai dressing, or grilled rib-eye with wasabi sauce. Cocktails prepared by mixologists moonlighting from Hyde & Seek Gastro Bar (see p040) include the Bangkok Mule — a blend of Mekhong rum, lemongrass and ginger ale. *111/2 Soi Ari 4, Thanon Phahon Yothin 7, T 02 619 6886, www.saltbangkok.com*

Long Table

Since opening in 2008, Long Table has
become one of the city's top nightspots.
An entrance corridor, which is illuminated
by hundreds of spotlights, leads into the
main room and its 25m teak centrepiece
(left), which can seat up to 70 people
and is reckoned to be the world's longest
dining table. Conceived by the design team
behind Bed Supperclub (see p054), here,
too, divans are placed at the edges of the
room, and are frequented by beautiful
jet-setters and wealthy Thais. Located 25
floors up, Long Table's expansive windows
have views of Benjasiri Park, and there is
an outdoor terrace with a pool and cocktail
bar. The Thai cuisine is equally impressive
aesthetically, although it can seem like
a vast triumph of style over substance.
25th floor, Column Tower, Sukhumvit Soi 16,
T 02 302 2557, www.longtablebangkok.com

INSIDER'S GUIDE

PIM SUKHAHUTA, FASHION DESIGNER

Bangkok native Pim Sukhahuta deeply treasures the city that, indeed, treasures her; she is renowned locally for the whimsical womenswear she creates as head designer of Sretsis (Second floor, Gaysorn, 999 Thanon Phloen Chit, T 02 656 1125). Sukhahuta trained at New York's Parsons School For Design, but her heart brought her home. 'Everything is so flexible here and you can have an easy life,' she says. 'It has all the convenience and excitement of the modern world, as well as the traditional charms of Thai culture.'

Of Bangkok's culinary scene, Sukhahuta says: 'The food is great and so cheap you can eat like royalty.' Her top venues are Quince (see p038) and Vanilla Garden (see p073), or, for sushi, Isao (5 Sukhumvit Soi 31, T 02 258 0645). A night out might start at sake bar Hotaru (3/1 Sukhumvit Soi 51, T 02 261 6660), followed by a visit to WTF (see p058) next door. If she has the energy, Sukhahuta will end up at late-night bar Wong's Place (27/3 Soi Si Bamphen), watching music videos till the wee hours. Come daylight, friends join her at the Talad Rot Fai market (Thanon Kamphaeng Phet) to hunt for vintage treasures. Otherwise, Sukhahuta may view an exhibition at Kathmandu Photo Gallery (87 Thanon Pan, Thanon Silom, T 02 234 6700) or RMA Institute (Soi Sai Nam Thip 2, Thanon Sukhumvit 22, T 02 663 0809). 'There's such creative diversity and so much emerging talent in Bangkok,' she says.

For full addresses, see Resources.

ARCHITOUR
A GUIDE TO BANGKOK'S ICONIC BUILDINGS

Of all the dirty, congested, unplanned metropolises in Asia, there is none more inspiring than Bangkok. If it wasn't for the manner in which its highways, municipal structures and 1960s bungalows all collide in a mad, buzzing pile, the city wouldn't be where it is now: teetering on the verge of a new movement in design (and, one hopes, architecture). Modern Bangkok is chaotic at first, but well-patterned at a distance. The 18th- and 19th-century wooden homes and old palaces are remnants of the last fluid era in Thai architecture. Since then, Western and Thai elements have fused, a trend that reached its zenith with the Dusit Thani (see p012).

Monument malls continue to sprout in the suburbs, yet the likes of Duangrit Bunnag's H1 (opposite) and the Face Bangkok complex (29 Sukhumvit Soi 38, T 02 713 6048) are indicative of a 'boutique' backlash. Of more recent developments, the SkyTrain, which was extended in 2012, stands out for its transformation of urban space. Further additions to the skyline include Raimon Land's double-tower residential building The River (13 Thanon Charoen Krung) in 2012, and the mixed-purpose Central Embassy (Thanon Phloen Chit/Thanon Witthayu), due for completion by 2014. For now, the city may lack a single architectural moment to put it on the world design map, but it does force one to see things differently, and in a very Thai context.

For full addresses, see Resources.

H1

Although many of his very best works are private or outside Bangkok – such as the tranquil Hôtel de la Paix (T 032 709 555) in Cha-Am, 160km to the south – Duangrit Bunnag is fast becoming Thailand's first truly great modern architect. H1 is his reshaping of a mini-mall in the buzzy Thong Lor neighbourhood. At night, when the interlocking L-shaped structures are lit up, the open-box architecture makes this a great place to wander around. All the Bunnag signatures – the division of public and private space, the touch of tropical Zen, the incorporation of a centuries-old tree at the centre of the compound (above) – are there. To Die For (T 02 381 4714), an H1 restaurant and lounge with a courtyard, is a charming place from which to ponder the scene. *988 Sukhumvit Soi 55*

Elephant Tower
A testament to the locals' appreciation
of all things bright and eye-popping,
Arun Chaiseri's 1997 Elephant Tower
arguably could not have been built
anywhere else. Its leg-like pillars (which
house offices and apartments), pinkish-
grey exterior and cut-out eye might come
across as gaudy elsewhere, but in a Thai
context they have a camp, quirky appeal.
369/38 Thanon Phahon Yothin 26

Democracy Monument
Completed in 1939, the Democracy
Monument, which sits in the middle of
a busy roundabout, commemorates
Thailand's first constitution, signed on
24 June 1932. To signify the date, each of
the four 'wings' stands 24m tall – their
height makes them a useful navigational
aid while you get your bearings in the city,
although the traffic around the monument
can make it difficult to see it up close. The
design was by an Italian, Corrado Feroci,
who became a Thai citizen and was even
credited with launching the country's
modern-art movement. His huge granite
statement became a rallying point for
civil unrest, and the tragic consequences
of protests in the 1970s and 1990s have
imbued it with a rather more solemn
impact than its creator intended.
Thanon Ratchadamnoen Klang/
Thanon Dinso

Bed Supperclub

Designed by Orbit and finished in 2002, this restaurant/club (see p054) is an other-worldly creation made of various metals and polymers. Neon shades of blue, pink, green or orange glow from within; video installations adorn the inner walls. The whole building can be moved on a truck: a beautifully crafted comment on the city's transience.
26 Sukhumvit Soi 11

SHOPPING

THE BEST RETAIL THERAPY AND WHAT TO BUY

Style has become Thailand's greatest form of modern capital. The fake Fendi and low-cost Lacoste that once pockmarked the street markets finally seem to be on the wane. This has been helped by a variety of government initiatives. The Thaksin administration (2001-2006) sought to promote the city as a fashion hub, which also sparked heavy government investment in film, graphic design and other creative industries. Trailblazers include H Ernest Lee, owner of H Gallery (201 Sathorn Soi 12, T 08 021 5508), and Sretsis, helmed by designer Pim Sukhahuta (see p062).

The most popular and reliable crafts to seek out in Bangkok include the minimalist, earthen ceramics, all things graphic, and jewellery – whether it's the dramatic ethnic selection by Kit-Ti's Jewelry (T 081 173 3884; by appointment only), or former Comme des Garçons collaborator Ek Thongprasert's playful rubber-clad pieces sold at Club 21 (Second floor, Erawan, T 02 250 7719). Retail outlets are often destinations in themselves, as is the case at multi-label boutique Code 10 (First floor, Siam Paragon, 991/1 Thanon Rama I, T 02 610 8312) and the outrageous vintage mash-up It's Happened To Be A Closet (266/3 Siam Square Soi 3, Thanon Rama I, T 02 658 4696). At the upscale Crystal Design Center (1420/1 Thanon Pradit Manutham, T 02 101 5999), more than 10,000 Thai and international design brands have a colourful presence.

For full addresses, see Resources.

Vanilla Garden

Occupying a converted 1930s house that now consists of two Asian eateries and the Sauce bookshop (above), Vanilla Garden is owned by Visaka 'Jom' Raiva. The store has a double-height glass front and is set beside a pristine garden, at the centre of which sits a tall fountain. The interior displays difficult-to-find and specialist tomes on subjects ranging from Indian cooking to architecture in modern China; rich students and the wives of Japanese expats are among those who are found browsing here. The complex is also the location of the kitsch, 1950s-style Vanilla Café, which serves hearty Japanese fare and pâtisserie, and the Chinese restaurant Royal Vanilla, where diners tuck into dim sum while seated on wooden stools. *53 Ekkamai Soi 12/Sukhumvit 63, T 02 381 6120, www.vanillaindustry.com*

We*Do Gallery
The brainchild of architect Markus
Herchet and interior designer Francisco
Polo, We*Do Gallery sells a well-curated
selection of furniture and fashion by
the design glitterati, including Asplund,
Maison Martin Margiela, Muuto and
Moroso. Home fit-out consultations are
also on offer, and rotating art exhibitions
qualify the 'gallery' aspect of the title.
79 Thong Lor Soi 8, T 02 391 4866

Flynow III
Few Thai brands can boast the success
of Flynow. Its catalogue of retail outlets
and diffusion lines includes Flynow III,
which subverts the label's signature
monochrome clothing with floral-print
dresses and colourful tote bags pitched
at a young female market. The Central
World store has an antique wood finish.
Central World, 4/5 Thanon Ratchadamri,
T 02 646 1037, www.flynowbangkok.com

Harnn

When it comes to Thai-style wellbeing, it's hard to beat an indigenous massage, but the land of lemongrass has much more to offer the body. We picked up these natural soaps (above), THB170 for 100g, by Harnn, a local brand that's stocked in 14 countries. Vitamin E-rich extracts of rice-bran oil (an antioxidant with both moisturising and anti-ageing properties) provide the core ingredient for Harnn and its sister brand Thann's (see p094) wide range of natural hair, body and skincare products for men and women. Harnn's Bangkok flagship (opposite) opened in 2005 in the Siam Paragon complex, and was designed by managing director Vudhichai Harnphanich, who was inspired by the appearance of traditional herbal medicine shops.
Fourth floor, Siam Paragon, 991/1 Thanon Rama I, T 02 610 9715, www.harnn.com

Propaganda
Launched in 1994, Propaganda is revered
for its cutting-edge product design,
especially the glossy plastic pieces with
humorous touches. Many, such as the
stools shaped like molars, are inspired
by anatomy. The store is dominated by
a foam model of the brand's chirpy Mr P
logo, which hangs from the roof.
Fourth floor, Siam Discovery Center,
Thanon Rama I, T 02 658 0430

Almeta

Although most people flock to the Jim Thompson House (T 02 216 7368) in their blind, giddy rush to tick silk off their shopping lists, several more personal (and singular in terms of style) alternatives are more consistent with the current Bangkok trends. Almeta is a one-stop shopping affair for bespoke silk design that has been going strong since 1992. In the two-storey house, designed by co-partner Hugh Zimmern, customers can choose any combination of weave, ply, weight or colour that they desire, subject to a minimum order of 20m if the fabric isn't already in stock. As all items are hand-woven on request in Almeta's Isaan factory, in north-eastern Thailand, goods can take up to three weeks to complete. *20/3 Sukhumvit Soi 23, T 02 258 4227, www.almeta.com*

Lamont

Alexander Lamont founded his Bangkok workshop in 2000, and today the firm comprises a team of more than 170 artists, craftsmen and designers, specialising in Asian-influenced furniture, lighting and art objects with a craft background. The rosewood and shagreen 'Tree Table' (above), THB60,000, can be found at Lamont's flagship store (opposite) in Gaysorn, which opened in 2003. The interiors – all Thai silk panels and walls covered with textured grasscloth – are the vision of Hong Kong-based designer Stephen James. Adding to the line-up of Lamont outlets in Bangkok and Phuket, another store, designed by Peter Hunter, opened in the city at the Four Seasons (T 02 650 2668) in 2010.

Third floor, Gaysorn, Thanon Phloen Chit, T 02 656 1392, www.lamont-design.com

UnCENSORED

Shopping in Bangkok can be exhausting, but taking the legwork out of finding the style vanguard is multi-label boutique UnCENSORED, which offers clothing from all corners of the globe and caters to both sexes. Opened in 2010 at Central World, the store – originally created by Erix-Design – was recently given an interior realignment by local firm Be Our Friend. It is interspersed with numerous delicate touches, such as vintage Fontini light switches in the fitting rooms, and a muted Scandinavian-style simplicity. Head here to rub shoulders with fashion-savvy Bangkokians, who come each season to snatch up labels that are hard to find elsewhere in town, like PAM and Surface to Air. Time your visit right and you'll uncover seasonal limited-edition releases. *Second floor, Central World, 4/5 Thanon Ratchadamri, T 02 646 1448, www.uncensored-bangkok.com*

SPORTS AND SPAS

WORK OUT, CHILL OUT OR JUST WATCH

As chaotic and sweltering as Bangkok can be, there are calmer intervals, when pockets of breeze and gorgeous light make for a great time to exercise. Cycling tours have become popular, taking in a maze of the city's backstreets. Try a route offered by Amazing Bangkok Cyclist (10/5-7 Sukhumvit Soi 26, T 02 665 6364), then mix with fellow pedallers at Aran Bicicletta (18 Ari Soi 4, T 081 821 9603), a bike shop and café. Gym time is a priority here and places like The Racquet Club (8 Soi Amara 3, Sukhumvit 49/9, T 02 714 7200) are scenes unto themselves. Yoga and Pilates are booming, and classes are affordable, whether you head to Lumphini Park (see p014), or to one of the many studios, such as Yoga Elements (23rd floor, Vanissa Building, 29 Soi Chit Lom, T 02 655 5671).

Muay Thai (Thai boxing) is a bloody, gymnastic spectacle and a centrepiece of Siamese culture. The best place to watch it is Ratchadamnoen Stadium (1 Thanon Ratchadamnoen Nok, T 02 281 4205); you can also get involved at The Siam hotel (see p018) which has its own ring. Golf is popular, and visitors who want to tee off should head to Muang Ake Golf Club (52 Moo 7, Thanon Phahon Yothin, T 02 533 9335), which has reasonable fees and is about 30km from the centre in Pathum Thani. And who could forget the form that Bangkok has nearly perfected? When it comes to urban day spas and massages, there's nary a bad one to be had. *For full addresses, see Resources.*

Divana Massage & Spa

Set within an idyllic tropical garden plot, Divana occupies a converted two-storey wood-and-brick house. It opened in 2002 and mainly caters to foreigners, especially those from Japan and Korea, who are keen to experience one of Asia's premier spa destinations. There are 15 individually designed Thai-style spa rooms, each with a private steam room and a small bathtub, as well as a dimly lit, teak-floored main area. Options include Siamese massage and a signature Milky Miracle head and body treatment, and prices range from roughly THB950 up to THB7,150 for the most expensive Ayurvedic package. Afterwards, relax with some herbal tea in the air-conditioned pavilion that overlooks the tropical gardens.
7 Sukhumvit Soi 25, T 02 661 6784, www.divanaspa.com

SF Strike Bowl

Bowling has been co-opted with style in Bangkok. This particular outlet is secreted away near a food court on the hectic top floor of the MBK Center, and was designed by Orbit Design Studio, the team behind Bed Supperclub (see p054) and Long Table (see p060). The highly graphic style and pale minimalism – incorporating wooden floors, greyish-blue walls and white ceilings – are quite similar here, and the decor adds a certain panache to the proceedings. There are pod-like karaoke booths, a DJ stage, sleek lounge areas and even shoes specially designed by Orbit's creative team. Opened in 2003, the success of SF Strike Bowl has been such that there are now six further branches in the city, each bearing Orbit's signature.

MBK Center, 444 Thanon Phaya Thai,
T 02 611 7171, www.sfcinemacity.com

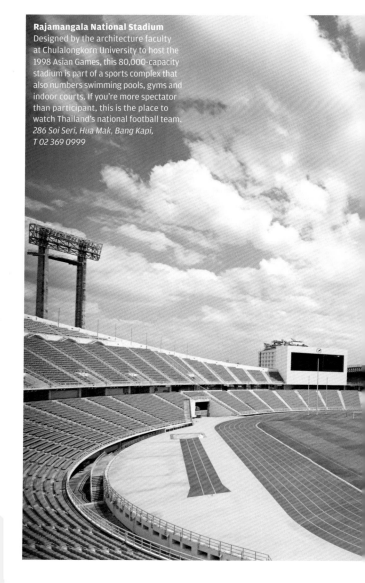

Rajamangala National Stadium
Designed by the architecture faculty
at Chulalongkorn University to host the
1998 Asian Games, this 80,000-capacity
stadium is part of a sports complex that
also numbers swimming pools, gyms and
indoor courts. If you're more spectator
than participant, this is the place to
watch Thailand's national football team.
286 Soi Seri, Hua Mak, Bang Kapi,
T 02 369 0999

Thann Sanctuary Spa

We've been buying Thann's natural wood-infused shower gels and jasmine-scented hand creams for years and were first in line when its spa opened in 2005. It offers a wide range of holistic treatments, including Ayurvedic head massage and a signature antioxidising treatment based on Shiso leaf extract. The interiors, a mix of Zen and tropical influences, are by founder Tony Suppattranont and designer Vitoon Kunalungkarn, and have a dark-green-and-brown colour scheme that evokes the rainforest. The 6m-high ceiling is adorned with 12,000 pieces of bamboo. Six low-lit treatment rooms are themed by the brand's product range – Rice, Aromatic Wood, Oriental Essence and so on – and are fragrant, moody and suitably sensuous. *Third floor, Gaysorn, 999 Thanon Phloen Chit, T 02 656 1424, www.thann.info*

ESCAPES

WHERE TO GO IF YOU WANT TO LEAVE TOWN

Paying due respect to the Thai love of extremes, if one leaves the sprawl and traffic of the city, it will most likely be for some kind of peace and a touch of nature. You could drive the 90 minutes north to the UNESCO World Heritage temples of Ayutthaya, or head west, where the seven-level waterfalls of Erawan, idyllic river scenery and the Bridge on the River Kwai lure coachloads to Kanchanaburi. However, in our opinion, the best option is to do as most locals would when given the chance – go to the beach.

It isn't always necessary to go all the way down to Koh Samui, Phuket or Koh Chang for exotic scenery. Bangkok is, after all, a port, and the placid Gulf of Thailand is just an hour's drive away. Take a trip to Koh Samet, a beautiful island and national park approximately 200km south-east of the city, which is, by turns, a party destination, a quiet respite or a family gathering place, depending on the chosen beach. For convenience and style, the best destinations are Hua Hin, thanks to Anantara Hua Hin Resort & Spa (43/1 Thanon Phetkasem Beach, T 032 520 250), and the town of Kui Buri (opposite). The former was once a fishing hamlet, but entered the spotlight when King Rama VII built a palace there. It has since become the Hamptons of Thailand, attracting a glitzy weekend crowd to its spread of great hotels, seafood restaurants, summer jazz festival and elephant polo tournament.

For full addresses, see Resources.

X2 Kui Buri

In recent years, the cluster of villages situated around the once sleepy town of Hua Hin, 270km south of Bangkok, have seen an influx of jet-setters. A number of cutting-edge resorts have now opened in the surrounding area, at beaches such as Pranburi and in the pristine town of Kui Buri, a three-hour drive from the capital. This is the setting for the original outpost of X2, the design-led Thai resort company owned by the Boutique Hotel Management Asia group. Twenty-three stylish villas stretch across four acres, each featuring bare rock and a glass front wall. Most accommodations have private pools, and four are on the beachfront, including the Luxury Pool Villa (above). A bar and restaurant offer sophisticated sustenance. *52 Moo 13, Aoi Noi, Muang, Prachuap Khiri Khan, T 032 601 412, www.x2resorts.com*

Six Senses Yao Noi

For a picture-perfect luxe-out, visit Koh Yao Noi, just east of tourist-frenzied Phuket. Here, Six Senses' 55 unique villas, designed by Habita Architects, offer sea or mountain views, as well as a private pool and butler. The spectacle of vertical limestone pinnacles, just off the island's coast, is not to be missed.
56 Moo 5, Tambol Koh Yao Noi, Amphur Koh Yao, Phang Nga, T 076 418 500

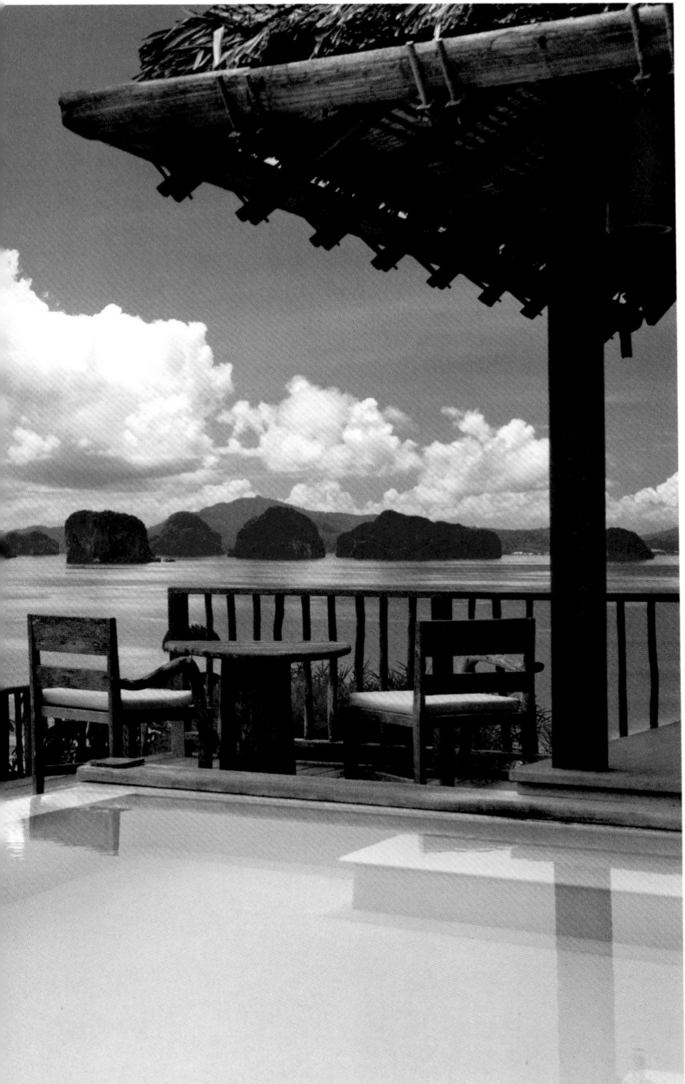

The Library, Bo Phut, Koh Samui
On Chaweng Beach, this fun, literary-
themed resort, the brainchild of interior
designer Tirawan Songsawat and owner
Kasemtham Sornsong, centres on
a striking glass-fronted building that
displays a range of art and design tomes.
The 13 suites and 13 studio cabins have
a bold red, grey and white colour scheme
and many come with ocean views.
14/1 Moo 2, Chaweng Beach, T 07 742 2768

Casa de La Flora, Phang Nga

Set on a tranquil beach north of Phuket, facing the Andaman Sea, this modern complex opened in 2011. Its 36 cubist villas, designed by VaSLab Architecture, feature pools and cloistered outdoor areas, and have large windows with clear views of the ocean. Inside, rooms are furnished in teak and quartz, and boast custom-made furniture with organic floral motifs by Anon Pairot Design Studio. Stay sequestered by day, then at night dine under the stars on the restaurant's beachfront terrace. Thirty minutes away, and accessible by shuttle, the resort also has its own private enclave and pier, Stella de Silva, where guests can kayak, swim and fish on a canal. Cooking classes and yoga lessons are also offered here. *67/213 Moo 5, Khuk Khak, Khao Lak, T 076 428 999, www.casadelaflora.com*

NOTES

SKETCHES AND MEMOS

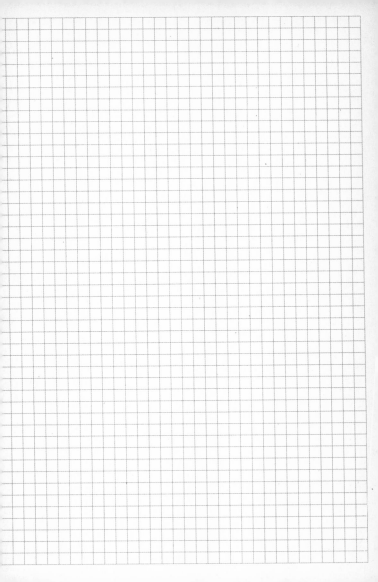

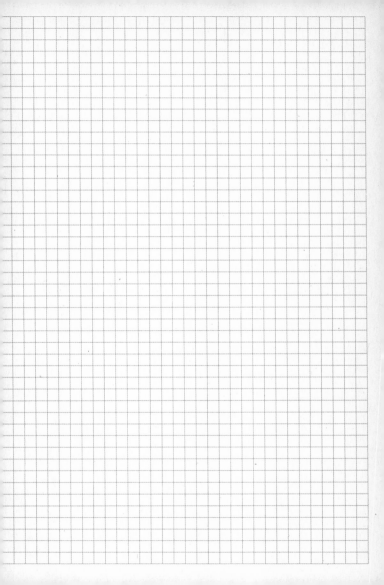

RESOURCES

CITY GUIDE DIRECTORY

A

Above Eleven 040
 33rd floor
 Frasier Suites Sukhumvit
 38/8 Sukhumvit Soi 11
 T 02 207 9300
 www.aboveeleven.com

Almeta 082
 20/3 Sukhumvit Soi 23
 T 02 258 4227
 www.almeta.com

Amazing Bangkok Cyclist 088
 10/5-7 Sukhumvit Soi 26
 T 02 665 6364
 www.realasia.net

Aran Bicicletta 088
 18 Ari Soi 4
 T 081 821 9603

B

Bamboo Chic Bar 044
 Fourth floor
 Le Méridien
 40/5 Thanon Surawong
 T 02 232 8888
 www.lemeridienbangkokpatpong.com

Bangkok Art and Culture Centre 037
 939 Thanon Rama I
 T 02 214 6630
 www.bacc.or.th

Bed Supperclub 054
 26 Sukhumvit Soi 11
 T 02 651 3537
 www.bedsupperclub.com

Bo.lan 053
 42 Soi Pichai Ronnarong
 Sukhumvit Soi 26
 T 02 260 2962
 www.bolan.co.th

C

CAT Building 010
 72 Thanon Charoen Krung

Central Embassy 064
 Thanon Phloen Chit/Thanon Witthayu

Club 21 072
 Second Floor
 Erawan
 T 02 250 7719
 www.club21thailand.com

Code 10 072
 First floor
 Siam Paragon
 991/1 Thanon Rama I
 T 02 610 8312

Crystal Design Center 072
 1420/1 Thanon Pradit Manutham
 T 02 101 5999
 www.crystaldesigncenter.com

D

Democracy Monument 068
 Thanon Ratchadamnoen Klang/
 Thanon Dinso

Divana Massage & Spa 089
 7 Sukhumvit Soi 25
 T 02 661 6784
 www.divanaspa.com

D'Sens 042
 Dusit Thani
 946 Thanon Rama IV
 T 02 200 9000
 www.dusit.com

Dusit Thani 012
 946 Thanon Rama IV
 T 02 200 9000
 www.dusit.com

HOTELS
ADDRESSES AND ROOM RATES

Anantara Hua Hin Resort & Spa 096
Room rates:
double, from THB3,760
43/1 Thanon Phetkasem Beach
Hua Hin
T 032 520 250
www.huahin.anantara.com

Arun Residence 020
Room rates:
double, from THB4,000;
Roof Garden Suite, from THB5,800
36-38 Soi Pratoo Nok Yoong
T 02 221 9158
www.arunresidence.com

Cabochon Hotel 017
Room rates:
double, from THB4,200;
Suite, fromTHB5,600
14/29 Sukhumvit Soi 45
T 02 259 2871
www.cabochonhotel.com

Casa de La Flora 098
Room rates:
villa, from THB12,000
67/213 Moo 5
Khuk Khak
Takuapa
Khao Lak
Phang Nga
T 076 428 999
www.casadelaflora.com

Chakrabongse Villas 027
Room rates:
double, from THB5,620;
Garden Suite, THB11,200;
Thai House, THB14,000;
Riverside Villa, THB16,850;
Chinese Suite, THB28,000
396 Thanon Mahathat
T 02 222 1290
www.thaivillas.com

Dream 030
Room rates:
double, from THB2,500;
Dream Suite 807, THB10,000
10 Sukhumvit Soi 15
T 02 254 8500
www.dreambkk.com

The Library 100
Room rates:
studio, from THB15,000;
suite, from THB17,000
14/1 Moo 2
Chaweng Beach
Bo Phut
Koh Samui
T 07 742 2768
www.thelibrary.co.th

Luxx XL 016
Room rates:
double, from THB2,000
82/8 Soi Lang Suan
T 02 684 1111
www.luxxxl.com

Mandarin Oriental 016
Room rates:
double, from THB12,900
48 Thanon Charoen Krung/Soi 38
T 02 659 9000
www.mandarinoriental.com/bangkok

Metropolitan by COMO 026
Room rates:
double, from THB4,500;
Terrace Room, THB12,400;
Penthouse Suite, THB25,000
27 Thanon Sathorn Tai
T 02 625 3333
www.comohotels.com/metropolitan

Millennium Hilton 016
  Room rates:
  double, from THB5,350
  123 Thanon Charoen Nakhon
  T 02 442 2000
  www3.hilton.com
Hotel Muse 016
  Room rates:
  double, THB4,720
  55/555 Soi Lang Suan
  T 02 630 4000
  www.hotelmusebangkok.com
Hôtel de la Paix 065
  Room rates:
  double, from THB5,600
  115 Moo 7
  Tambol Bangkao
  Amphur Cha-Am
  T 032 709 555
  www.hoteldelapaixhh.com
The Peninsula 016
  Room rates:
  double, from THB8,000
  333 Thanon Charoen Nakhon
  T 02 861 2888
  www.peninsula.com/bangkok
Shangri-La Hotel 031
  Room rates:
  double, from THB7,415;
  Speciality Suite, THB111,815
  89 Soi Wat Suan Plu
  T 02 236 7777
  www.shangri-la.com/bangkok
The Siam 018
  Room rates:
  suite, from THB16,300;
  pool villa, from THB31,000
  3/2 Thanon Khao
  T 02 206 6999
  www.thesiamhotel.com

Siam@Siam Design Hotel & Spa 024
  Room rates:
  double, from THB6,590;
  Grand Biz Class, from THB9,180
  865 Thanon Rama I
  T 02 217 3000
  www.siamatsiam.com
Siam Kempinski Hotel 022
  Room rates:
  double, from THB5,870;
  Garden Suite, from THB20,900
  991/9 Thanon Rama 1
  T 02 162 9000
  www.kempinski.com
Six Senses Yao Noi 098
  Room rates:
  villa, from THB17,300
  56 Moo 5
  Tambol Koh Yao Noi
  Amphur Koh Yao
  Phang Nga
  T 076 418 500
  www.sixsenses.com
Sofitel So 028
  Room rates:
  double, THB7,000;
  Water Rooms, from THB8,900;
  Wood Rooms, from THB13,800;
  So Lofty Room, THB26,000
  2 Thanon Sathorn Nua
  T 02 624 0000
  www.sofitel.com
Sofitel Sukhumvit 016
  Room rates:
  double, THB6,000
  189 Sukhumvit Soi 13-15
  T 02 126 9999
  www.sofitel.com

X2 Kui Buri 097
Room rates:
villa, from THB12,500;
Luxury Pool Villa, THB30,000
52 Moo 13
Aoi Noi
Muang
Prachuap Khiri Khan
Kui Buri
T 032 601 412
www.x2resorts.com
W 016
Room rates:
double, from THB5,200
106 Thanon Sathorn Nua
T 02 344 4000
www.starwoodhotels.com

WALLPAPER* CITY GUIDES

Executive Editor
Rachael Moloney

Editor
Ella Marshall
Authors
Richard Mcleish
Adam Renton

Art Director
Loran Stosskopf
Art Editor
Eriko Shimazaki
Designer
Mayumi Hashimoto
Map Illustrator
Russell Bell

Photography Editor
Elisa Merlo
Assistant Photography Editor
Nabil Butt

Chief Sub-Editor
Nick Mee

Editorial Assistant
Emma Harrison

Intern
Charlotte Tillieux

Wallpaper* Group
Editor-in-Chief
Tony Chambers
Publishing Director
Gord Ray
Managing Editor
Oliver Adamson

Contributors
Arglit Boonyai
Rob McKeown

Wallpaper* ® is a
registered trademark
of IPC Media Limited

First published 2006
Revised and updated
2010, 2011 and 2013

All prices are correct at
time of going to press,
but are subject to change.

Printed in China

PHAIDON

Phaidon Press Limited
Regent's Wharf
All Saints Street
London N1 9PA

Phaidon Press Inc
180 Varick Street
New York, NY 10014

Phaidon® is a registered
trademark of Phaidon
Press Limited

www.phaidon.com

A CIP Catalogue record for
this book is available from
the British Library.

ISBN 978 0 7148 6606 2

PHOTOGRAPHERS

Jeremy Woodhouse/
Getty Images
Bangkok city view,
inside front cover

Alex Hill
Robot Building, p013
Arun Residence,
pp020-021
Siam@Siam Design Hotel
& Spa, pp024-025
Dream, p030
Wat Arun, pp034-035
TCDC, p036
Sirocco, pp048-049
Bo.lan, p053
Long Table, pp060-061
Vanilla Garden, p073
Flynow III, pp076-077
Propaganda, pp080-081
Divana Massage
& Spa, p089
Rajamangala National
Stadium, pp092-093

Jason Michael Lang
Siam Kempinski
Hotel, p022, p023
Erawan Tea Room, p033
D'Sens, pp042-043
Nahm, pp050-051
Tables, pp056-057
H1, p065
SF Strike Bowl, pp090-091

Elisa Merlo
Harnn soaps, p079

Robert Polidori
CAT Building, pp010-011
Dusit Thani, p012
Shangri-La Hotel, p031
Elephant Tower,
pp066-067
Democracy Monument,
pp068-069

Marc Schultz
Lumphini Park, pp014-015
Chakrabongse Villas, p027
Nest, p052
Salt, p059
Almeta, pp082-083
X2 Kui Buri, p097

Christopher Wise
Cabochon Hotel, p017
The Siam, pp018-019
Sofitel So, pp028-029
Bangkok Art and
Culture Centre, p037
Quince, pp038-039
Soul Food
Mahanakorn, p041
Bamboo Chic
Bar, pp044-045
Smith, p046, p047
WTF Gallery & Cafe, p058
Pim Sukhahuta, p063
We*Do Gallery, pp074-075
Harnn, p078
Lamont, p084
UnCENSORED, pp086-087

BANGKOK

A COLOUR-CODED GUIDE TO THE HOT 'HOODS

CHATUCHAK
There's more to see here than the market, especially at night when this area comes alive

OLD TOWN
Where Chinatown met luxury hotel development and lost. The Chao Phraya is fascinating

SUKHUMVIT
Not so much a district as a traffic-heavy thoroughfare. Pick your stopping points wisely

SIAM
A study of shopping contrasts: slick malls to one side, neon-lit alleys to the other

SILOM/SATHORN
Gay bars, lady-boy shows and fine restaurants all lie close to the city's financial heart

ROYAL CITY AVENUE
Open until late, this former student haunt has been transformed into clubland central

For a full description of each neighbourhood, see the Introduction.
Featured venues are colour-coded, according to the district in which they are located.